The Pendulum

The Pendulum

New and Selected Poems by

Robert Watson

Louisiana State University Press *Baton Rouge and London*

1995

Manufactured in the United States of America
First printing
04 03 02 01 00 99 98 97 96 95   5 4 3 2 1

Designer: Glynnis Phoebe
Typeface: Baskerville
Typesetter: Moran Printing, Inc.
Printer and binder: Thomson-Shore, Inc.

Library of Congress Cataloging-in-Publication Data

Watson, Robert,   1925–
        The pendulum :   new and selected poems   /   by Robert Watson.
        p.   cm.
        Includes   index.
        ISBN 0-8071-1972-5 (cl).   —   ISBN 0-8071-1973-3   (p)
        I. Title.
        PS3545.A874P46   1995
        811'.54—dc 20   94-31288
                                                                                  CIP

The author offers grateful acknowledgment to the editors of the publications in which some of these poems first appeared: "Nomads," *Laurel Review,* XXIV (Summer, 1990); "A Balloon Rises" and "Teresa and the Spear of Time," *South Carolina Review* (Fall, 1992) and (Fall, 1994); "My Father Breaks His Hip at Eighty-One" and "The Cure," *Greensboro Review* (Summer, 1989); "Judgment Day at the Library," *Omega News* (March, 1990); "The Great Wall," *International Poetry Review* (Fall, 1990); "Dogs," *Tar River Poetry* (Spring, 1990). Many of the poems in this volume have previously appeared in collections of poetry by the author: *A Paper Horse* (New York: Atheneum, 1962), copyright 1962 by Robert Watson; *Advantages of Dark* (New York: Atheneum, 1966), copyright 1966 by Robert Watson; *Christmas in Las Vegas* (New York: Atheneum, 1971), copyright 1971 by Robert Watson; *Selected Poems* (New York: Atheneum, 1974), copyright 1974 by Robert Watson; *Night Blooming Cactus* (New York: Atheneum, 1980), copyright 1980 by Robert Watson.

Publication of this book has been supported by a grant from the National Endowment for the Arts in Washington, D.C., a federal agency.

The paper in this book meets the guidelines for permanence and durability of the Committee on Production Guidelines for Book Longevity of the Council on Library Resources. ∞

For
Gavin Keens and Benjamin Keens
Margaret Watson and Elizabeth Watson

He made darkness his secret place;
his pavilion round about him were dark waters
and thick clouds of the skies.

At the brightness that was before him
his thick clouds passed, hail stones and coals of fire.

David

The poems in this volume are printed roughly in chronological order of original publication, with the exception of "Watson on the Beach," the final poem, which was first published in 1962.

Contents

Contents

Contents

The Pendulum

An Elderly Ghost Has His Say

This Halloween I'll just stay put at home.
An old ghost, my grave grows on me: warm shrubs,
An oak, asters, my flesh their sap, their leaves,
And their dead leaves my food; my voice the owl,
Wind or what I choose. I am content,
Content as I was never home in life,
My restlessness, mind scattered, gone to seed.

It took some getting used to I'll tell you.
At first my wet best suit began to shrink
And I swelled up like biscuit dough until—
The bone, wood box split. And I was born again:
A child playing in dirt, his parents gone.
Worst was that stone men stuck on top of me—
To keep me in, remind me of my name—
Heavy as my memory of childhood,
Weighed down with that trash they teach in school,
But the oak kicked down, weeds ate up the stone.
Here it's mindlessness that counts. A fleshpot
I was and am. You should have seen me glow
In youth, this youth with neighbors' bones
Dancing, mingling in the dark. But that's behind,
Behind me in my wild phosphorescence.
A ripe corpse now of two hundred Halloweens,
I find this grave is good enough for me.

Gossip has it my wife has turned black cat.
Agnes was always bad luck, bad luck for me,
Licked clean in her black Sunday dress she wore
To church to purr, claws closed in her black muff.
She thought she'd be a spirit when she'd die.

1

A spirit? When I'm solid as a mudpie.
To be dead you can't be squeamish, must be
A part of what Agnes could never bear.

Some lovers hide near graves as I once did,
Impatient, wanting my hard earned change,
Straining an hour in my lap; find, weep
That all this buckling on another fails.
Here it is our nature, law: I am my neighbor.
I am worn thin with what men above call sin.
Even in my dust age lust blows me on
To lace with other flesh, birds, beasts,
Grass and men. In spring a child once came here
And ate a wild strawberry at my foot.
And ate a little part of his great, great
Grandfather's left big toe. Do you smell smoke?

In fall when boys play with matches in the leaves,
Piled as comforters for my snug winter's nap,
I turn nervous, fear fire spreading out of hand
In which I die again, not to be buried
In cool moist ground, sweet darkness of earth's flesh,
In which I mix, change each day, spread my arms
Out to the living world which lives in me:
My nightmare is fire that burns me to the clinker
Men call soul, and I am tossed to heaven,
Hell—who cares?—some other birth far away
From ashes of my accustomed lover earth;
To sit with that creature who was my wife;
To burn forever in fire of her yellow eyes,
Raked by metal claws: a mouse that black Agnes
In her superiority would have had me be.

✦

The Judge Winds His Clock

The Judge is dead.
The Judge is dead.
Throw him out the window
And spit on his head.

Each week I deal out years of jail.
Each year discard a life or two.
Each day for lunch a salad bowl.
(He sliced her head off in a fit;
She'd hid his shoes to keep him home)
Two bourbons evenings, never more.
I bathe at nine, I bed at ten,
I play croquet, cards, fish for trout.
(Law allows twelve fish in season)
The crimes men do. I see them all.
By now a million years of jail.
Inside a house, a cell of chairs,
We plotted crime 'til father set
Clock, wound sun, stars: his sentence bed.
Over our house, our cell, our crime,
The Grandfather's clock turns his face
To us, chimes his sentence for lunch,
 Bourbon, bed, childhood, discarded lives.

All rise, eyes on me in black robes.
I strike my gavel, over-rule,
Spin lawyers through my wickets, thickets.
And ORDER, ORDER in the court.
But could they see me in the bath
Where I stand, mirrored wet on scales!
Justice weighs itself, a fat fish

Of sixty: *Two hundred and four.*
This can't be me. Did she look so
When my morning's criminal struck
Off her head? Fish are not human.
And criminals? And I? I am a lover . . .
Of cards, croquet, the clock, and order,
Order in the court. I yearn to be
What I am, in robes . . . my bathrobe.
I take comfort in numerals.

The clock ticks like a heart. My heart
Ticks like a clock. Ice in my glass
Of bourbon clicks like dice. I shake
My fortune, my head. Grandfather chimes.
It's ten. I lock doors, windows,
Shut opinions in a briefcase,
Wind up Grandfather for tomorrow's
Judgment day. All is in order.
My wife completes her crossword puzzle.
The clock ticks. Dark. And all is well.

Swimming in bed I hear a noise.
Did I leave the faucet running?
Under the clock I hear a humming,
A stream flowing, line going out.
A feathered lure sinks through the ceiling.
Someone is trolling. I am dreaming.
I hear the clock and know it's raining.
Stars swim through wickets on our lawn.

Above the Supreme Court meets,
The Chief Justice, who wears no shoes,
Is setting the sun in his eye.
He strikes a ball through the wicket,
Winds his nose with a cloth. A cold
Today? What struck is now stricken.
And listen! The clock, the judge, says,
"Twelve."
         "Twelve what?" I ask. "Twelve fish
In season?"
         "Just twelve!" Chimes the Judge
In his bathrobe and whacks the bench.
So it is. I roll in a ball.
The gavel strikes. My sentence dealt . . .
A million years and lives discarded.
It rains outside the house, the jail,
And order, order in the court.

✦

Whore with Trick

I let him in my room, lock the door;
Then lock the door of the room inside my head,
Where he tinkers, puffing at the knob,
Stoops peering at me on the bed,
Peering for what he, what the world thinks I have hidden.
I must call the janitor for more weather-stripping
The wind is puffing through the cracks,
And chills my bones outside the door.

Now I lay me down to replay movies in the head-room
Caught in snatches between times when I am paged
By that usher selling candy with the curls,
Who hustles on my errands in a limousine I tipped him,
When another lady
Seeking servants in the theater caught his eye.
O I play on film a lady of leisure,
Retired, tired of my lovers
Whom I cut like sausage links.
As a rich lady I have seen,
Done all there is to do,
Seen all the stars playing,
Replaying under the lid where I have something I must hide.

In my travelogue you see me kiss the Pope
In my black sheath mourning . . . but mourning what?
I seem to have lost connection
At the Ladies House of Correction.
But here at St. Peter's on our screen
I light a Roman candle for a body that is dead.
O the candy butcher sent me pills
For the common female ills,

And kept me in good humor
When the doctor cored my "tumor."
So I light a Roman candle for a body that is dead.
In a lap dissolve I rocket on to Spain
To catch the ears of the matador
The bull will gore and throw to me,
Then the candy butcher and I can celebrate,
Eat oysters incognito at the Ritz—
As rich as Rockefeller—
In a suite of all black marble
Where I have something in a trunk that I must hide.

Now the reel seems out of order,
Projects blackness on the screen.
In the jungle night I hear a puffing,
A tinkering with a camera or a fuse,
And I must hurry, run bury what I have hidden,
But where, but what?
A shot! Loud as the door that slams,
And all that puffing, the tinkering stops,
Sound runs off its tracks
And silence cracks from the ceiling,
Until I am buried, trapped in my movies
After my theater has failed.

Yet squinting at my sockets, pointing sockets
To the keyhole of the room outside my room,
I see diamond rings are counting money in my purse,
And now I see a powdered face, familiar curls and fists
That batter, battering the door of the room that is my room
Until the door springs in. Thank God.
Here's the candy butcher. Light on, night done.
I'll stop the blood and put the coffee on.

But now I remember what I have hidden in the room
That is my room.
I have a closet, inside a trunk, inside a jewel box locked
That has a secret drawer,
And in the drawer, wrapped in tissue is a heart-shaped locket.
In the locket, if I alone unlatch it,
Is a magic mirror in which I can make myself appear.

✦

Odalisque

How negligent they appear in this north light, our light,
Falling liquidly with dust from those high transoms,
Spilling over her form, still as a bowl of fruit.

She rests naked, carelessly it seems, on her side.
A long loop of pearls drops down over one breast,
Repeating the loop. Her pedestal, a couch draped
With a dusty cloth, stands before a flower papered wall.

From his easel, he contemplates her; she does not notice him.
She thinks entirely of herself, and he entirely of her.

Cold air and light roll and flash over her form,
Pour around looping lines of flesh that waver
Below her dispirited eyes. Her right nipple stiffens,
Gathers itself against the tide. Elbow, shoulder, back
All ache, constrain to hold her form in stillness,
To hold her body in suspense against the crushing sea.
She lies aching and arched, negligent and beautiful
Before the trembling green of an imaginary garden
Under surging lights on a cloth of red and saffron.

Her eye catches a glint of pearl; she thinks, unthinkingly,
Of her own pearl skin—a Venus bedded on a fanning shell;
Again she must feel that she is beautiful, an object of art
And adoration, her fire our light. But in her vanity
Does this elemental woman dream that she is everything,
The model of the universe, these pearls the stars
Of her heaven? If she feels this in her unthinking
Self-concern, why does she look dispirited then,

Like some bead-telling nun in sleep? Does she gazing
On her flesh think of approaching death? On viewing
Her pearl skin, that wedge of darkness at her thighs,
Does she despairingly sense the history of the womb,
Those ancient shapes winding and unwinding on its floor?
And looking on her breasts recall the fruit she ate
When time began . . . ? No. How can one so carelessly composed,
Stretched out on that dusty coverlet of fading red,
Ponder such thoughts in this cold north light?
What she dispiritedly ponders, we cannot know.
Yet she is the secret model of our dreams who guides
All wanderers in sleep: arched in stillness,
Beautiful, negligent before moving light of day.

Sirens in the street ruffle the stillness in the room,
Embroiling molecules of air; yet neither hears.

He stands, idly it seems, a brush dangling from his hand.
The canvas at his easel is blank, flat, white space.
He contemplates her; she does not notice him.

He stands against light and noise thinking of her
As yesterday he thought of oranges in a bowl.
Mapper of half-known spheres, oranges and women,
He loves neither, but uses both to quench a double thirst,
To wet a double palate. To him the spheres of each
Are always new and changing, yet the same and still.
Our galaxies—like floating trees—drift, bloom, give birth
And die in an endless sea of space, and she on the couch
Floats drifting, changing among flowers of the sea.
Not all his art can seem to fix, to still her shifting form;
Not all her art can still her shifting form for him,
Or calm the running sea of air and light in which she moves.

In anger at disorder in the light, his hand tightens
On the brush, ready to assault the space, to fill,
To flood a canvas with the wildness of this turning room.
But then, perhaps, he calls to mind some day of serenity
When a woman naked on a couch, an orange in a bowl
Were shadowed and still, quietly geometrical,
Glowing somberly like last coals dying in a grate.
And that he must have thought was long ago, before his time.
Yet now somehow she settles down before his eyes . . .
She drifts into the garden, her swelling breasts flatten
Among leaves and flowers. She becomes the papered wall . . .
To him warring air and light remain without the scene,
As if a glass door framing her were shut and he stood
Out in a storm gazing in upon her sleeping form;
And he can no longer separate looping lines of flesh
From looping of flowered paper, spread, or beads.

He holds a knife now, loose, it seems, in his hand.
With one swirling gesture, as a master skater on new ice,
He cuts in wood one long looping line, a few swift arcs,
And he is done. Yet his canvas remains blank, flat, white space.

She rises aching from her pose of negligence,
And covers breasts which in her standing seem to droop.
We see that she is neither beautiful nor young.
Without a glance at him or his work, now dressed she leaves.

The print is black, a few thin lines of white cut in black
A figure of a woman sits, not lies, with one elbow
On her knee, a string of pearls orbited about her hand,
Flowers looping around her form. This place contains no light
Or shade, seems nowhere we have ever been. And she?
She is supported, indifferently, by nothing we can see:

A black flower arched on a flowered wall of black.
In one corner hangs a blossom, its lips open over her head.
Inside the blossom we see nothing but darkness . . .
Unhuman woman, if woman at all in a world not seen
Even in our dreams, yet a world that must be everywhere—
We will suspend you in our rooms and meditate
Upon your simple shape winding there among the flowers.

Old oranges in the bowl glow like coals, fade to shadow
And go out. Light from the transom windows, our north light,
No longer spills over bowl or couch. All light is out.
He has gone. Yet in black stillness the scent
Of turpentine and oil moves into the invisible stream of air,
Spreading out the transom windows, and rolls slowly
Toward the scent of onions frying on a floor below.

◆

A Paper Horse

Tonight the world's roof burns,
The yellow roof of the last palace of a living God
Blackens in my dreams: my spirit shrinks in bed.

How childish habits persist! In bed before sleep
I unfold my mind's map in the dark and mark
A place to sleep, a tent near Lhasa,
Where in the distance I see the gold-roofed Potala.
Within the God-King, a boy,
Sleeps in one of its one thousand rooms,
Or wakeful, watches his subjects through a telescope.

In bed before sleep I journey to Tibet to sleep.
In mountain climbing gear, I rise through snow,
Lean into the winds of invisible Everest,
Rest on a gorge's frozen lip, dream there
Of the Abominable Snowman on whose lip, perhaps, I lie;
Then slide, now in real sleep, down a glacier
On the mountain's other side,
As a child on my sled I coasted in Passaic
At night down Aycrigg Avenue, and at the bottom,
By a bonfire, my father stood to take me home to bed
And dreams of coasting down a steeper hill.

Tonight the world's roof burns.
God, a youth in glasses, flees on horseback;
Among sword swinging Khambas circles north,
And at the sound of shots, or demons, stops.
His fur-capped lords then serve him buttered tea.
They wait, twist turquoise earrings, huddle against mules.

But now the oracle speaks, his astrologers concur.
They turn south, wade over drifting snow, scale
The kingdom's ice-faced walls and down;
God descends from his heaven of snow and stone,
From his last kingdom, his last palace,
Where on the roof, still burning, his bodies,
Salted, boiled in butter, face with gilded eyes,
The snow and smoke packed wind. Nearby,
A priest snips paper horses for lost travelers,
Last travelers, loosens them in the wind,
Turning prayer wheels,
Turning oak leaves outside my bedroom window,
Turning clothes on the line my wife has forgotten.

✦

Callers

"May we visit you, Miss Burckhardt, my dear?
Come from behind the blinds you peer through.
Telephone and doorbell ring and ring,
You have spent your lifetime in not answering.
Now callers you should not ignore are here."

"I will go on unanswering all each day.
Silence! While I add infernal taxes up—
Federal, state, city grasp and grasp
What I have spent my lifetime saving.
Wolves at my door, callers, away, away!"

"We have come for you, Miss Burckhardt, my dear.
Not money hidden as refuse, breeding,
You have spent ninety years concealing
Under your sink, bill upon bill upon bill.
Now callers you cannot ignore are here."

"Will telephone, doorbell, voices never cease?
All night the beech tree knocks at my window,
Wind at door, rain at roof, dust at floor;
I can scarcely total numbers anymore.
When will you give, O Lord, this servant peace?"

"We must have you, Miss Burckhardt, my dear.
Take from your dresser that old brown sock,
Where you keep your house and strong box keys,
Limp on your cane, unbolt the triple lock.
A thief? Behold, I stand at the door and knock."

The knocking and ringing and calling at last
Shook up her head like a dynamite blast.
She limped to her dresser, to her sock for her keys.
She unbolted her door, but saw nothing there,
Not caller, not thief, not tree, dust, nor air.

✦

Her Father Is Drunk in the Graveyard

A hand of stone on top of a tipped tomb
That pointed up to heaven once now points
Straight at my father's slumber where he lies drunk
In wet grass in shade of an upright tomb.

My father's fingers point along the grass
At nothing—unless at a dove who died
Under a bush, its wings outstretched, head squashed,
With father's empty bottle lying beside.

Age or vandals with these slabs have played
In time a crazy kind of dominoes;
Yet no one comes to straighten up the rows
Of tipped or leaning stones where father sleeps.

* * *

When they stretch together in wet grass,
Each pointing toward the other, I see
That stone and dove and man's ends are the same—
What father knew too well would come to pass.

No middle for him: a beginning and end,
An unending ending of his waking life,
A shade drawn daily against the living world,
A walk in blindfold to a borderland,

Where this stateless man sees, or dreams he sees,
The soft, welcome shadow of his lover
Waiting, secret on the river's other bank,
Arms outstretched, beckoning him softly over.

And there he lies peering over the water,
Weeping, without a passport for his crossing,
Lies on the edge pretending he is dead,
Ears stopped to cries of wife and daughter.

* * *

Do all men stray to dark, beyond our cries,
Fiddle with death, and listen to music played
By instruments of their sober trades:
Lawyers drawing wills, the surgeons knives?

Did these vandals race to end of reason
To find life under this life, and dig hard?
Or did they in wild love turn up the yard
To show us nothing is here, nothing at all?

For my husband let me have the vandal
Who will outrage the other life and leap in this,
Who will topple tombs and outrun scandal—
Beat Death in dominoes before we kiss.

* * *

Dear dreaming, wasted Father, floating
Further each day from my hardening memory,
I will let you slumber here, let you lie
While I move further from you tenderly.
O my dear dying, drunken Father, go floating
Softly to her dark, winged kingdom waiting.

✦

The Child Raper of Chelsea

I've lived by washing filth away,
Dishes, pots, pans for forty years.
I fill garbage cans with bones.
All I touch soiled, spoiled: the world.

Why should I buy false teeth? I had
No appetite for food; I drank instead.
I tried, I tried: I changed my job
A dozen times each year, each time
Back to sinks again. Between jobs
I washed, rinsed myself in gin
And beer until the smell was gone,
Until I could not see my hands
That wiped the filth away. Content?
Almost content. "A little love?"
The women laughed. My teeth, I guess.

I saw her playing hopscotch.
I said, "Come and see my sick child."
I was the sick child on the bed.
A naughty girl to go with strangers!
She screamed. You tell me now she's dead,
Will never smear lipstick on cups
That I must clean. Poor, pure child.
I could not see my hands that day,
Those days I broke a hundred plates.
I loved her and not meaning to,
I saved her from the worst fate: life.

Monster, you say I am, but she
By the Mass of Angels is free
Of this filthy world, by me.
Father, I've scoured the world for Thee.

✦

Advantages of Dark

The sun
Through cold slabs of air
Over a slice of field
Between prongs of leafless oaks
Through the double-glassed windows
Through thick oil-heated air
The sun snaps at you
Asleep on the bed
On the tan rug
On the oak floor.
Light thrusts
At your body
Chalks flesh in parts
Snips shoulders
Neck
Unstitches hair from skull
Shears head from pillow
Cuts out eyes
Divides your lips
Splits you from me.
Night assembled us
Drew my limbs to yours
Molded us to the bed
Clamped bed to floor
Floor to frozen ground
Bedding the dead
Holding the leafless oaks
Night spread us with black
Seeded with stars
To warm our bed.

                    Until scissors of light
                        Shears air from field
                            Oaks from windows
                Cuts you from me
                    From the bed
                        Bed from floor
                                Dissects you to particulars
                                Thumbs toes knees eyes hair
                        Snips you from the unborn
                The living and the dead.
Light holds
        More mystery than dark
                Light cuts
Like a child
        With blunt shears
                Cuts
                        From an old magazine
                The pictures
        From the pictures
Name by name.

✦

Going Nowhere Alone at Night

All houses stand in pools of black.
A police car's blue roof-eye trails
Me down this Fall night of drifting
Leaves. I drift. I drift. It's wrong
To fall in love so many times,
So many times. The yellow leaves
This Fall more beautiful than last.

They curb me with a siren cry.
"Destination? Your license please!"
"Nowhere. I can't sleep." O the stars
Warm, luminous as . . . It's wrong
With half-dressed trees so lovely now
As you and they were and all are.
The blue light spins away in leaves.

Why don't I root myself in bed;
A black tree in rows, unmoving,
Of black trees? It's wrong to fall in love
So many times, so many times.

✦

The Marksman and His Game

He *would* notice her.
First afar, in his eye like a speck of dust.
Then nearer planted in the doorway of his sight
Until she would be a custom to his eye.
Sudden absence next!
He'd puzzle if his front-yard tree ran off.
And return, return gliding in circles
In loose clothes like long plumes.
He would wonder what foreign bird this was.
He would raise his eyes like barrels of a gun,
And when his eyes were aimed, she would hover
Without a smile, or frown, would turn to him
Her eyes open windows to a dim fire-lit room.
Then close; with lowered head she'd pad away.
She'd never have to listen to his talk:
His feet would tell her scuffling through the forest
To her porch. And quiet, quiet. Words his weapons
Would never do. He'd scatter shot into the night,
Open the door, reach under and stroke the heart;
Then he'd skin her by the fire, but she'd poke him in the pot.

✦

Victory

Moving furniture around my room
I can move stars, the streetlights and the dust
In rolls below our chairs. I can change weather
If I want.

Changing the order of books in shelves
Christ marries Helen, Alexander leans
On Mother Goose. I can change all history
If I wish.

Putting on clothes I have not worn before
I sit on a shifted chair turning my body
To something new. I can be President
When I choose.

Opening the door to watch the snow
I walk frozen ground, past frozen trees,
Around the block, around. I can circle the universe
When I will.

Indoors I light a fire to warm the air,
I can move the chimney across the room,
Or doom the furniture in the hearth
If I please.

But you, like a frozen tree in frozen ground,
I'll walk around, I'll walk around the block,
I'll shift all the furniture in my room.
I'll move you yet.

✦

In the Drugstore
(Five Nights Before Christmas)

The girls twist the radio
Until it squawks,
Something to do, to do, to do, do, do.
BONG swings the fist of the clock.
The druggist winds up a toy panther;
The black beast climbs a wire tree.
Then one girl swings the druggist
In dance until girl two
Flips out his wide red tie for something to do.
They run out, shout, "Old lecher, old goat";
And his bought squirrel teeth smile back
Saying, "Not one drug works."
SNAP goes the front door lock.

Two girls kick at the streets,
Frown in windows
Until their feet hurt worse than their hearts.
To do, to do, to do, do, do.
In her own home in bed
Each peers into a black sheet, her heart.
The black sheet rises, and each trembling asks,
"Is there a black panther loose in the dark?"
No. The black sheet risen shows
A widow sipping tea
Watching boxes wrapped for grandchildren
Under the Christmas tree.
A red squirrel stares from the almond-laden sill.
Each sighs in sleep, "Is that widow me?"

But Night stays up pacing the drugstore floor,
Frowns at the book, the magazine rack.
"I've read you all," says Night.
"For something to do
I'll dial Weather on the phone:
Night here, send me rush
Slush, sleet, then snow, and hard, hard blow."

The sick elm in front of the drugstore,
Alone without a bird in a limb,
Gives up the ghost, throws himself
Headfirst through the glass,
Smashing drugs, radio, clock.
Night, alive by a miracle,
Packs the one unbroken toy,
A black panther, in his bag,
Jumps over the fountain, the elm,
Black hat pulled down tight
Against the spreading light,
Hums,
Something to do, to do, to do, do, do.

✦

The Blue Whale

Three hugest dinosaurs do not outweigh
That one hundred foot long whale who will strain
The sea for krill, four tons a day. Svend Foyn,
A man, found how to blow its twenty pound brain
To rice and still its thousand pound heart
For its forty thousand pounds of oil. Soon
The blue whale fewer than the whooping crane
will be, who is a useless bird. Of old,
Churchmen said the devil was like a whale.
Soon we can sail dry seas empty of all
Monstrosities, and man alone can strain
The little krill, all food, thought for his brain.
There's life some say in smallest grains of rice.
Man must eat; killing is not good, not evil.
After waters are plundered well as land,
I will think
Of Svend Foyn who destroyed the devil,
A one hundred and fifty ton, toothless blue whale.

✦

Lines for a President

The Inauguration and Shortly After

You could not stop the snow the sky dumped down,
The cold, the lectern smoking when the priest
Invoked the Lord. Did the Lord in answer jab
Your poet blind? Was that your high silk hat
They held against the sun for Robert Frost?
And still he could not see his words for you.
Coatless, then, as if winter were not here
You blow cold words, your hand chops air.

Your wife's French chef breaks skulls
Of eggs. Upstairs her dresser
Gardens in her hair.
A maid brings scented pearls,
The world of Louis and Molière,
Her conquest of Versailles
And Athens. Downstairs
You praise the Spartans.

At the Funeral

Let all those who would stop a war
Sit in a chair and rock
And stare at a woman with flowered hair;
Have her chef prepare
A banquet for all the heads of state:
Let them advance between the Spartan guards,
And past the priest and past the poet.
Let the music play, have them dance,
And rocking in your rocking chair,
Point to a state of possibility:

The fragile arts of peace
Shatter the weather of war.

Now six grey horses draw you to where you are,
Not to Versailles, Sparta, or Athens.
The seventh horse is wild and black
And riderless and paws the streets of Washington
Where you are rocking and will always rock.

John Fitzgerald Kennedy,
You could not stop the shells,
The drowning of your boat in war;
You could not stop the snow the sky dumped down,
The cold, the lectern smoking when your priest invoked
The Lord, your poet struck blind, the bullets in your head,
The six grey horses drawing you to where you are
Rocking and will always rock.

The seventh horse is riderless, wild and black.

◆

Riding a Motorcycle

on Halloween
(How near the dead the children seem)
Past skeletons, witches, and ghosts,
All children among the night-lit orange
Of pumpkins, leaves, my cycle coasts.

Shall I frighten the dead back to bed?
A roar. One more scorching up the road
And done. Dead leaves, the dead, like blood
On my hair, a crown my stiff fingers
By our porch's pumpkin-light I shed.

I pull blinds, blow out our pumpkin.
Our unmasked, exhausted children sleep.
Then down the chimney, or my mind,
Close-mouthed ghosts float in procession.
Around the living room they bend,
And near the end I think I see
Both our children, my wife and me.
A sip of cider clears my head
Of all nonsense about the dead.

I need not cycle to arouse
Or drive back the dead who nurse
Me with cider pressed of the fruit
From our apple tree's now bare arm
Burning in the fireplace. Up, out
The chimney sparks fly like stars. Warm
Stars fade with sparks. I float to sleep.

Is nothing private in our house,
Nor in the grave, nor universe?

✦

How Cunning of Them

                    each morning
To stick the live, the dead oak up
Outside my window when my eyes
Come unstuck, before my feet hit
The floor to unroll the lawn—brown—
Unpack the fence, the house next door,
Let down one of their skies (Today's
Is soot grey), spray in temperature,
Hand out noises to the children,
Give me a beard before I get
To the mirror over the sink.
And the way they bring the air back!
It beats me. All night they subtract,
Pulling mean tricks, like sending you
To work without your pants, shooting
At you, even burning down the house.
Once they struck me with a lightning bolt
On the stairs. I knew I was dead.
I did a circus front flip landing
On my head, but it didn't hurt.
I was pleasantly dead a second,
Then they rushed back the windows
With the live, the dead oak glued on
And I unstuck my eyes again
And made darn sure I got my pants
Put on, belt and buckle put on right.

◆

On Stage, Off Stage

I've buried Troy, I've conquered Rome
And Hollywood. My crown, my head
Roll in a trunk with other parts
I wear. This is the good Lord's beard
I wore the day I made Adam,
Adam's fig leaf when I was he,
My horns for Mephistopheles . . .
Hamlet, Vanya, Lear, and Faust
Lie here. I shut the coffin's lid.
Curtain down, clothes, lives removed
I search the program for my name
In vain. What was it? I don't know.
Another life, name so long ago.

Find the birthmark on my elbow,
Tell me the nurse's error,
Of a changeling. "You are, you are . . .
The eldest son, the only heir . . . "
Curtain before he tells my name.

No more of men, no more of gods,
The dreams of men, the dreams of gods.
No more of parts, of parts of parts
Made up by men who made up life.
I'll play spaces between stars,
Dust rising from dancer's feet.
The world sprouts from my trunk, my limbs.
My leaves, our stars whisper: "You have
No name."
    I am now satisfied.

✦

Success

There must be something more than this,
Having whatever I wished to have,
Kissing the woman I wish to kiss
In this dark weatherless room,
In this wide, placid pond of bed
Shored with books, papers, pills, cash;
Our children safety stored, both wed;
And I insured against all loss,
Catastrophe.

Customarily
My doctor sends me bottled sleep;
Everything so right, I want wrong.
I can't worry about the bomb;
All my named fears now long gone,
I almost wish a war again,
Where I can crouch behind the lines,
Listen to crack of shells as then;
My feet blistered in frozen boots.
Gone the first sweet match, first drunk,
First unfaithfulness. The worst,
The best over, done. Every dream
Of swimming, I swam, but the one
Up that last black, blank sealed
Stream.

Once on a tour of Rome
I saw Him swim from Chapel's roof,
Cracked, peeling; saw angels burst
Through wood, stone until I almost,
Almost . . . No; friends, wife would grin.
Smothered in our seasonless air,
Anchored in this tepid pond,
In Eden, innocent, ignorant,
Sane,
                    how can I complain?

✦

Commuting

Here at the end of the line
The night's final train stops;
In the last car the dark drops.
Here at the end of night
A clock shrieks, the wife shoots flak,
The children detonate on my back.
And red morning (Where is that sock?)
And red morning streaks in ringing:
O sweet ambulance of dawn.
Here at the wall of my desk
I command the envelopes away:
Hup. Two, three, four,
Fire the directives out the door.
I scream at the waitress to bring my bill.
O sweet salad why doth thee lie so still?
Here at the edge of the track
The hearse stands to take me back.
Listen, the wheels do snap and rave
Until at the edge of the grave
Where dark is as sharp as a knife
I flop in the tomb of my wife.
Here at the opening gate
I board a windowless car.
With the hiss of a connubial snore
It moves as slow as a star.

✦

Christmas in Las Vegas
(A Widower Speaks)

I shake its arm, the dials spin,
My life in bells, oranges, lemons, bars turns.
I can't lose, I can't win.
The hours shuffle by metallically here
Where neither night nor day nor hours are
Where under the pink, blinking bulbs
Over the fields of green felt
No one is young, no one is old.
The breasts of chorus girls swell like boils.

I bought a girl with chips last night.
O Doll, the beauty parlor styled your hair in pewter,
 With lotions and light they plated your body with brass
Ignoring two white circles of breast
And one white stripe of ass.
All night we whirred and clicked
Bells, oranges, lemons, cherries, bars.
Assembled for departure in your blue fox
Your look pretty as any juke box.

I am a machine facing a machine.
I insert a quarter, shake an arm.
My arm is a handle, my legs are steel.
The dials of my mind spin.
I can't lose, I can't win.
My throat chokes with coins,
I spew quarters from my mouth.

Alone unriveted in the bath
Under the steady neon
A beast hisses, shakes its furred head.
I look out the window with my wolf's eyes.
It is night. It is night.

I have been a beast, I have been a machine.
Rabbit's foot and four-leaf clover, for Christmas
Let me hit the jackpot: make me a man
Who can hold a woman in tenderness,
Bear memories of tenderness,
Make my life in winter midnight moonlight spin
Where I will lose and I will win.

✦

Nostalgia of the Infinite

Flags fly from a white tower's top in a green sky.
The dark couple at its base do not embrace,
Look up or down. This is the nostalgia
Of the infinite,
Of the infinite set on the retina,
On the base of the brain when the rain wipes clean
The brain pan and the wind bangs the pan on its nail.

✦

Two Strangers in a Motel Room

HE

If I showed you my Matisse nude hung
In orange light shed from my oriental rugs,
My rare books, my Savile Row suits
You would begin to know the man I am,
The man I have unzipped and neatly spread
Upon the chair, the man that even now
You hear I cannot shed, that grows back
On me when I speak. And you, now you
From the orange light behind my eyes become
That Matisse nude. Stay as you were, *as you;*
And peel me back again.
Hold my flesh as a wand and with your flesh
Transform us until you and I are
Nobody in any motel room anywhere.

SHE

Let me be that Matisse nude in orange light
In your living room with your rare books,
You in your London-made suit. Carry me
With your voice from this room, from my room at home
With children's crayon scrawls across the walls,
A torn, toy-splattered once-green rug and me
In my last year's Sears and Roebuck pattern dress.
Press my breasts, my thighs to canvas thinness,
Whisper in my ear so that I know the man
You were, tell me
I am lovely, make your embraces lift me
To your orange light: a memory
From my long drive home from Mother's grave,
Your long drive home from wherever you came.

◆

Afternoon and Evening

The movies are grinding love upon the screen.
I think that I might scream.
I heard love long ago
Driveling from my radio.
Stared at by advertisements from a bus
Of chewing gum, a teeny tiny truss,
My wanderlust has lost its lust.
Here lies a lady under my subway car
Who leapt and stalled us all at 14th Street.
(I can see nothing but her stockinged feet)
At my side I hear the fat
Soprano of a passenger:

"Screwing, I said to him, what's that?
Why not? Who cares? Screwing don't touch me, I said,
And what do you know he wouldn't do it to me."

Christ, I need a day off.
Christ, I need a day off.
Christ, I need a day off.

The fire engines sing a funny song.

It was terrible, the swelling, the squeezing,
          All that pushing and shoving
On and on.
          And the strain, the breathing,
Not knowing when it would end.

The mind going cockeyed,
      All that pushing and shoving
On and on.
      The pulse skipping, pores opening,
It was terrible.

And tired as if we had been grave digging
      All night long, on and on.
Then the hammering, and teeth slashing
      In the black heat,
The endless tunnel.

It was terrible all that:
      They call it love:
That's what it was, on and on . . .

The fire engines sing a funny song.

◆

The Glass Door

Was I moving through the invisible glass
    Between life and death,
When I walked through the glass door
    I thought was open?
The glass fell on me like icicles or knives,
    My clothes turned red and then my eyes.

After the nurse sponged my face the surgeon
    With needle and thread
Mended me as if I were a tattered coat.
    "You will be the same as ever
After a month on crutches and two with a cane."
    But I am not the same.

I would have sworn our sliding glass door was open,
    Nothing between in and out.
In daylight I walk as a man in darkness
    Hands out to feel
What the darkness holds, to test for walls
    That shatter,

For invisible curtains between what we see
    And what we think we see
On rainy nights staring beyond the windshield
    Or out the kitchen window
Washing glasses in the sink. Telescopes are useless.
    Everything we cannot see is here.

✦

The Radio Astronomer

A radio astronomer in Utah lifts his ears
Over the moon and stars, sets them at empty space.
It's 3 A.M., a quiet hour. Beneath the moon it snows.

He sets his tape recorder to the ears, takes a coffee break,
Looks out the door at unintelligible random snow,
Its soft sound, drifting, each flake gorgeous as a number

In flight, gorgeous as stars and planets, their slow sounds
From long ago, cries amplified of stars in flight,
Sounds of the dead, the untranslatable tongues

Of the universe, where life other than this may be
Or was, surely, somewhere among the galaxies a signal
Could he hear it, in some recess a sound of familiar life.

Again he listens: the sounds seem random, or does he hear
A wheel turning, the click of dice, noise of cards dealt out?
A casino in the heavens? The powers wagering there?

He listens, tries to tie furniture of our lives
To each separate sound, sound to sight. The dice fall again.
The roulette wheel spins, slows, stops on an invisible number.

These sounds bring no grand music, no vision that Milton
Or Michelangelo knew. He unwraps a sandwich,
Pours more coffee. The sounds, he thinks are random:

This is a universe of luck and chance. Galaxies
Spin in flight like snow, rattle in space, are gone.
For a while light lives, sound lives

Spinning through valleys and mountains of empty space:
God in sound, the great gambler sending in flight
The dice, the stars, the snow at 4 A.M. in Utah.

At 5 A.M. home through snow in bed he touches the breast
Of a galaxy, hears the dance of the heart and the lungs,
Feels the cells gather and shower, his children waking.

The sun explodes in the bedroom. The universe
Is gone: He falls to a soundless sleep, a corpse.

◆

Planet Eight

We clambered down in airtight suits to the ground
Of Planet Eight where the temperature
For us was cold. The sky was green and windless,
Our feet sank into dust that felt like fur.

We marched toward mounds and tall stones we thought
Must be a town, marched through a plain of dust
Where nothing grew, no tracks of bird or beast.
Under the layer of dust was a crust

Of rock. Our mallets tapped the house-high mounds.
We bored holes. Our gloves rubbed dust from walls of stone.
We found no sign of doors, no carved words.
A light flashed from our capsule, then our phone

Clicked with orders to return. That was all
I saw on Planet Eight, that stillbirth
Or corpse: we would have welcomed rats or flies.
But on the long weightless flight back to earth

With my life's high point shrinking to star size,
I dwell on the dust, the stone mounds, a life
Without life. I land on our stranger planet:
I look out with hostile eyes.

◆

A Dream of a Dream of Night

Night won't leave me alone when I worn down
By Day who whips me through his hoops, his watch
In hand, when I undress for bed to read
In peace alone, Night pesters the door knob,
Stuffs sweet scented pollen under the sill,
And rubs her lips on my window whispering,

"*Come out. Come out. I'm raring to go.*"
"No. It's too late. I'm tired. No. No."
"*Please come out. We'll make love under my stars.*"
"Leave me alone. I've got a wife and child."
"*You coward, they can't see you in my dark.*"

There was no right answer I could make to Night
Except to leave the front door light burning.
I locked doors and windows tight, drew shades,
Too tired for yielding or not yielding.

It was late when I thought Night had gone.
When I fell in bed it was nearly dawn,
But under the bed clothes I felt a form,
Hair that was not Margery's on my cheek,
Stiff black hair across my mouth. "*It's me. Come on,*"
Said Night, "*I love you with all my soul.*"
And fell upon me like ten tons of coal.

✦

The Night Fear

I

First they stroke gently with hugs and sweet kisses.
   It will not go away.
Then they squeeze and suck, pinch the tender flesh.
   It will not go away.
They strike each other and bite until blood runs.
   It will not go away.
They lie touching without movement back to back.

It swoops and hisses over the dark room like a bat
   Or pendulum hour after hour
Over and over their still and sleepless limbs.
   "What is it?" "What's wrong?"
They ask themselves all the winter nights long.

At orange juice the children are lively as skyrockets,
   The furnace whistles, the dishwasher hums.
The *Morning Sun* says, STOCKS UP, WARMING AND CLEAR,
   CRIME DECLINES, PEACE NEAR.
The day spins on like a merry-go-round.

Undressed in bed, their light out,
   Like a bat or pendulum
Back it comes hissing through the room.

Yet all is usual: the clock nods on the mantel,
   A child coughs, a neighbor dog snarls.
In their bathroom a nightlight glows on the tiles
   And on the silvery medicine cabinet
With it useless ointments, drops, pills.

They plunge at each other, clinging, clinging.
   What is it? What is the matter?
Then the bed rises, they think, through the French doors,
   Soars up, up over the roof
Until below earth shrinks small as a ping-pong ball,
   And the Milky Way enfolds them
As if they float through an enormous Christmas tree,
   Invisible branches spangled with light.

Yet still back and forth like a bat or pendulum
   It hisses through the roofless empyrean.

Then as a toboggan the bedstead slides
   Down, down past the moon
Through the French doors back into their room.
   The clock nods, a dog barks,
The bathroom tile glows safely in the dark.

III

At night now, swooping over their forms, the fear
    Like a meteorite
Hisses over the room, over the house,
    Beyond earth's atmosphere
Back and forth, back and forth.
    No longer do they cling and bite
And ask "What is it?" "What is it?"
    They think, two in one bed in one room
Will always hear some unnamed noise,
    Some terror buzzing in their hearts or skies,
Some fear no love clasps can lock outside.

To sink in sleep each now pictures a skater,
    His face muffled, his long scarf ends streaming
And snapping in the crystal air,
    His heart racing, swooping and hissing
Over the frozen, star-pocked pond of night.

◆

High Dive

Twing.   Twing.   Twing.
                                     Splash!
An arc of flesh passes, has passed,
A head rises: over so fast.
Such grace, when others dive.

But I upon the plank tremble
A lifetime there. The pool,
Ten miles down, is dry concrete.
The upturned mouths, if I could hear,
Say "Die!" The next comes paddling
Up the rungs. "Die!"
                      Twing.   Twing.

I fling myself, my arms wings,
Then stretched, all stretched to needle
Sharpness. Nothing. Nothing . . .
Splash.

        My head rises
From my grave, from my bride.
I dry myself cocksure.
                      Twing.
Above me. My foot on the first rung,
In fear again my heart says
                "Die . . . Die."

✦

J. Goldsborough Bruff

Abandoned in the black unmapped unknown
Sierra Nevadas, my tent poles bend
With snow, so hungry I could eat my dog.
Instead of gold I dream of Indian
Stew. Nevada, pup, I wouldn't eat you.
You're too small. You'd make only one poor lunch.
The deer, the immigrants disappeared with snow,
All down the mountain. I am here alone
With wolves, ravens, grizzly bears. I am sick.
I live on venison-bone stew, with luck
A rare raven potpie. Under the snow
If I can find it, if I have the strength
To walk is a dead ox that I can eat.
My head aches, I have fever, hemorrhoids, sores
Open all over my body. The smoke
From my small fire chokes me, blinds me,
Yet in Washington platters heavy with food,
Logs blazing on the hearth, my children there,
I was dying of content. It was in
Dreams that I lived: The King of California,
Gold gushing molten from my mines' mouths; wagons
And ships heavy with ingots. How to live?
It was as if the wind tumbled me westward.
A tornado. I told lies to my wife.
"We will be rich," I said. And all along
I saw the flash of round plump gartered thighs,
Or black eyes of Indian girls I'd have.
Or sitting around the fire broiling buffalo
I'd shot, singing under the stars. All dreams!
We just took off like robins in the fall.
I thought I drove when I was driven west.
Ask me why I am here, I cannot tell.
I dine alone tonight on candle ends

So hungry I could eat up my best friends:
They died of cholera, scurvy, arrows.
And when wagons mired or their oxen died,
They burned the grain, broke their picks and shovels
So no one else could use them, poisoned wells.
They robbed, shot friends, dug up fresh graves for loot.
What would I do now? What *wouldn't* I do now.
I am J. Goldsborough Bruff, President
Of Washington City Mining Company
In my winter palace. Addressing my dog.

Too sick to travel more, left here to guard
Our gear. My men and passing immigrants
All promised to return for me, bring me food.
I'm just 32 miles from Sacramento,
But now the deep snowdrifts bury the trails,

And bury what they were and what I was
Or thought I was, and buried my dream of gold,
The triumphal march to the lake of gold
Led by our glorious President Bruff.
How the men hated me. How I hated the men,
Falling asleep with whisky during their watches.
And steal? They even stole my horse. And rape?
Indian women are ugly, such filth:
They are all a starving contemptible race.

Betrayed, Nevada, pup. Who are my enemies?
How can I curse the snow, the cold, the stars?
I have fallen lower than an Indian.
Could I have willed this end, frozen bones buried
In snow, my flesh down wolves' mouths? Map maker
How have I mapped my destiny? I have blamed

My men, I have blamed the snow, my own body,
These legs that won't walk. To be right in all,
And to fall to this. I have led my men
To doors of paradise. I am in Hell,
Alone where white and black are just the same:
Black sky, white snow frozen in darkness, me.

It's getting light, Nevada, up and out
Before the sunlight on the snow is blinding.
Up, if I can get up. Out, if I can . . .
I can. I walk like a man on stilts in snow.
My snowshoes are heavy as wagon wheels.
God give us game, give us firewood. Each way
I look trackless bare white snow, bare black trees.
I press a long pole through the snow again
And again week after week, a lifetime.
The light blinds me. I am one ache from head
To toe, one running sore. My pole has struck . . .
What? Dig. Dig. I dig with my hands. I feel.
Do I feel the rough frozen hide of ox?
I scrape and shield my eyes from burning snow.
I press my knife with all my weight and cut
Into the golden flesh of ox. I will
Return to Washington, rich, well, honored,
J. Goldsborough Bruff, mapper of the unmapped
West. The gold dust will fall like snow, my pup.

✦

The Last Wild Indian

For 4,000 years the Yani Indians, numbering about 300, lived an
undisturbed and unchanging life in a territory 40 miles long and 60
miles wide in the hills of northern California. In 1908 the white
men by slaughter had reduced the Yani to one man. This poem was
inspired by Theodora Kroeber's book, *Ishi in Two Worlds*.

In Golden Gate Park I watch buffalo
Or lie on my back staring with one eye
In my kaleidoscope, buy from a vendor
A penny whistle, then ride the streetcar
To what I call my home, my land, the museum
Where I am its chief exhibit, where I
Am an assistant janitor among crates
Of bones, among the debris of Egypt
And Peru, Greece and Rome. This is my home
On Parnassus Heights where on each Sunday
Afternoon crowds watch me shape arrow heads,
Arrows and bow, the last man of my tribe.

My body that has known no woman's body,
That lived for fifty years among the deer
And rabbits and otter, in winter clothed
With their skins, in summer bare, my body
Feels heavy in shoes, coats, the air heavy
With dead, the rooms with dead men's belongings.
We burn our dead. We keep no keepsakes, nothing.
Our land is perpetually clear, was clear
Until I saw as a child the White Man's
Demon that Mother said was the evil
That followed all White Men, the smoke and clank.
I burned my Mother's body when she died,
And lived three years alone until alone
Was worse than any evil. I gave up

To you who murdered my entire nation,
Who pamper me in this hall of the dead.
They called the Sheriff to the slaughter house,
Then jail, then the long ride in your demon
To the anthropological museum.
When you came in numbers we had not seen
We could not believe earth held so many men,
So many horses, cattle, mules and sheep
And guns to shoot us. We climbed far, high up
In hills away from you. And still you followed.
You did not kill us to eat as cattle,
You killed us to kill us. A noisy kill.
White men smell bad. Before we hunt to eat
We fast and bathe, our breaths clean as air was
In the stony hills, bodies pure of women.

Down wind, I whimper like a fawn or squeak
Like squirrels. Or with fingers on my lips
I make the soft kissing noise of rabbits,
The noise they make when frightened. The arrow
Is silent: The shaft's hazelwood, the feather's
Eagle: my bow covered with a lion's tail,
My quiver skin of one entire otter.
Behind a rock I whimper like a fawn,
I crouch. I listen and hear deer, and wait.
I smell deer. I whimper, and antlers show.
I whimper to draw the great buck up close.
In his eyes I see my eyes shine, and shoot.

My hands are four thousand years old, my hands
Can drill fire from wood, can twirl the man piece
In the woman piece until the sparks glow,
Can chip the heads of arrows from obsidian,
Can shape from mountain juniper a bow
Of such perfection that when I place bow
To my lips and tap the string it will sing

A melody. So more than anything
I love my bow strung with the finest thread
From long tendons of deer I chew and spin.
From boiled skin of salmon we cook our glue.
We waste nothing of what we kill. In fall
With squirrels we gather acorns for mush
To eat in winter in the warm huts where
Women shape baskets, talking their own tongue.
With us all must be clear: Your best drink: tea.
When the hot stones boil the venison stew
It is done: the meat firm and the broth clear.

In my bed in the museum I keep dreaming
Of winter in the hut for men. The sound
Of flint flakers, the tales of grizzly bear,
Or stories of Wood Duck Man, the great hunter
To whom women came: Waterdog Woman,
Waterbug Woman, Bat Woman, Fishhook
Woman, the eyeless Fox Woman, Mountain
Quail Woman, Brown Bear Woman with sweet roots
And herbs. Wood Duck would fling each out his hut
At dawn. Only Morning Star Woman stayed
Past one night, yet she could not catch the heart
Of that hunter whose arrows . . . I am dreaming,
I who have had no woman, will have no
Woman, no children . . . At times of evil
At moon periods, at times of evil blood,
The women lived alone in separate huts.
With sticks for digging the women would find
Sword fern, redbud, maidenhair, and all stems
And grasses for weaving baskets to hold
The nuts: hazel pine, buckeye—wild raspberries,
Huckleberries, plums and grapes the children
Would help to pick. The ducks and geese above,
We swam with flying salmon in their streams.
Our lives, rich, plain, turning as the seasons

Turned, at night under our open thatched roofs
We learned stories of stars, the Gods, our Gods.

Here in the museum in San Francisco,
In my new world, holding other old worlds
On Parnassus Heights, I look out the door
At the babble of people, trolley cars,
Autos, the roar of trains, a single plane
Above. I walk to the grocery store
In fog, in smoke, the street vendors clutch me,
So many people, so much noise. Should I
Return to my green hills, the soundless land:
Only bird cries, bees, wind, roar of a bear,
The music of water in which I swim?
In one pocket I have a penny whistle,
In another pocket a kaleidoscope.
Alone in the old world, alone in the new.
Dead in the woods my body would rot unclean,
My soul unclean, Here they promise to burn at death
My body, unlock my soul to shoot back
To heavenly fields of my tribe, my life.
I see through glass of the showcase I polish
The model huts, harpoons, baskets, arrows,
The feather robes. It is snowing. I join
Our father in a hunt for grizzly bear.
My name is Ishi, and Ishi means man.

◆

Off to Amazonia

I

In middle age
Take the car from the garage
In the garage with hammer and saw
With needle and thread
Build a boat, stitch the sails,
Stow corned beef, water, and rum
Sell the house before it's too late
Say "Good-bye. Good-bye."
We're off to Amazonia
The last vast emptiness on earth.

Whether to the moon
Or Amazonia
We sail into the past
The lizard watches the jet
Listen to the wind,
Take a fix from the stars:
Memory.

When I sit I am caving in upon myself,
Broken windows, broken steps, peach pits.

Collect the children
Buy the charts
And mark a route to Belem.

II

Will it be the same?
The roads billowing in red dust,
The armies of immigrants
Yellow eyed with dreams of gold,
Suffocating in the green sea of trees,
All ways pungent with dead animals and men,
Gun fire saluting a new civilization.

Through green rain forests
To grass plains and high table lands
With anteaters, deer, emus
Out of sight of the river
Out of sight of the small Indian tribes
To the land without borders
That is neither Brazil nor Bolivia, nor Peru
To the land oldest in emptiness
Where our faces in the water
Are the first faces the water has known
To the land fullest of all but men
The newest land.

The wind drives us over the black water.
The sun at noon is larger than earth.

Distance seeds the land of fantasy
It takes imagination to live at home.
Which is more daring: To stay? To go?
The white foam in the wake
The black waters at the prow.

III

In Amazonia we pick the ripe berries,
We rise at dawn, sleep when the sun falls
Swim naked. . .

Through the underbrush they come hacking,
The deer vanish to the sounds of axe and shovel.
At night cards shuffle
The breeze sweats tobacco and gin,
Blows to us the coughs of the dying.

Our boat is becalmed off Florida
The lights of Miami extinguish the moon.
Why do we want to be alone?
How long can we bear to be alone
On the sea, down the river, through the jungle?
What is hidden in the jungle?
Why do we hide in the jungle?

The divan on which I stretch is piled with pillows,
Indigo, silver, plum.
The children swim in the tepid waters of the bay.
I must rise to buy more gin and tonic
3 limes, 2 pounds of scallops
At night in the yacht club from my barstool
I hear the slap of baywater
The bar voices slosh in my ears,
My mind is at sea.

IV

We are not going to Amazonia
This year or next
The car still lives in the garage,
The boat, blueprints in an envelope
We are not going to Kenya or Tibet.
I test the bay water with my toe.

Lashed to my comforts,
I cling to the ordinary,
A mussel on a rock,
Hightide underwater, low above,
Nights. Days. Nights. Days.
The moon is as enchanting as ever.
Life is enchanting.

I lurch down the street on my sea legs
Casting invisible winks to invisible girls
I am off to Amazonia
Faster. Faster. The years—white foam in my wake.

✦

Mantoloking

Mornings in Mantoloking in sunny August are best
Immortal sea dotted with sails of white, white hulls,
                                                white foam
  Umbrellas, yellow, green, blue, a garden in eternal sand
Where gull and piper stand.

The houses of Mantoloking float on the sea
Great wooden arks with turret and filigree
Summer homes of the late nineteenth century rich
Whose architects dreamt of castles, shingle, porch
And glider. My grandmother, a young lady with parasol

(I imagine)
Strolls on the porch, her eyes on a white sail.
                        My grandmother died last year
At 94, and the houses of Mantoloking all sank
In the night in the sea.

◆

So, So

Do numbers torment him? I at least bleed.
He never says. I never say . . . beyond
"How are you, dear?" "Oh, so, so, so—so."
Bees never sting him mowing. I get stung.
I move my hands among kitchen knives, needles,
My trowel, the thorns of my roses, cats claws.
The cat purrs on his lap, never on mine.
"What's new today at the office?" "Nothing, nothing."
Our children live in envelopes that come each month:
They might as well live in graves for all
We know them now. For thirty years I've loved
Him. And he me. Or I wouldn't be here. Or he
Wouldn't be here. Apple of my eye, the smoke
Rises from his pipe. The newspaper waltzes
In his lap. My knitting needles go clickety, click.

I live among sharp points and cutting edges.
And he an actuary for Prudential Life
Lives in probabilities. Does he dream in numbers?
At least my needle pricking draws blood.
I know what hurts me. He sighs in the abstract,
Abstracted. I love him. I love him.
Just to hear him breathe or cough. I love him.
"How are you dear?" "So, so." I'll lock the door.
It's time for bed.

◆

Near You, Then You

I swallow my orange juice, I chew my toast.
I pray, I pray for a usual day
That moves routinely from stop to stop.
I read of a wreck on the IRT.
The elevator stops on the 30th floor.
Am I afraid of life or death or wrong?
If wrong it is? I dictate, "Gentlemen:
In the matter of . . ." Done. All is well, yet
I hear her typewriter play *liebestod*.
So reckless in dreams, compounded at six percent.
Is *LIFE* what others have? I have heartburn.

For eight years, eight hours a day, yet not touch,
Not say. And said and touched what then; what then?
My wife smiles up from the blotter. Noon time,
The straight and narrow I have followed narrows
To buttermilk, my cream cheese sandwich,
My untasted Jell-o. If I ask her
(Her glasses flashing in the haze of noon
Her hair gone from brown to grey), will she say,
Her vocal chords sweet as cello strings bowed,
"Oh love requited is love lost"? But still, still . . .
The stars are separate and the trees. What luck:
She here . . . at home a faithful wife and cat,
At home her needles go clickety-clack,
Here the keys go tat-ta-tat-tat.

In this sheltered world of home and office,
Office and home where lust and rage are banned
I lust and rage in wilds of sleep. Blessed
Are my days, this rich unvaried life.

✦

William Rimmer, M.D.
(1816–1879)

"Whose work is this?"
"No man's work," replied Drowne.
"This figure lies within that block of
oak, and it is my business to find it."
—Hawthorne

Anatomy is the only subject.
My father in this drawing has the nose,
The chin, the lobeless ears of Bourbon kings.
This is his cobbler's bench. He died of drink.
This silver flute he made to suit my voice.
I carved at fifteen the first undraped male
In the new world: it is father, the Dauphin,
In gypsum. I call it *Despair.*
How he feared the secret police of Talleyrand.
From France to England to Nova Scotia
To Boston. He knew the foot, this cobbler
King.

As cobbler, doctor, painter, sculptor,
I know the body, bones, muscles, all flesh.
I always fill the lecture hall. I know
The dreams, nightmares beneath the skull. I loved
Dissection yet art is over medicine.
Our form is not ideal but beautiful:
The Greeks got it all wrong. Take it as is
Is my motto. Job is my great hero: *is.*
My children's catechism is naming bones,
The bones with their light coats of flesh, the beast
Our minds forever battle: the contortion,
The final loss when body slain by sword
Or illness slays the mind. We all must fail,
Father.

And I looked at him with many
bitter thoughts as upon the son of
a king, wondering of his strange
fortune, who, knowing not his in-
heritance, was a gladiator having
no call but to shed blood at
another's will.

The Brahmin in Boston look down at me:
A cobbler's son, a king's grandson. The forms
I make of stone accurate to flesh, to dreams
Is not for them. They choose the Greeks
Where life is smoothed away. For them
Marble. For me granite, the hardest stone.
I have the lobeless ears of Bourbon kings.

◆

Paradise

always fades when we think of strawberries,
The first of a new spring or spring itself,
Entwined, we lovers, rinsed in warm white air:
Tulips strewing yellow and violet; lawn and trees
A green mist.

To think forever:
Lips sticky with strawberries, air sour with milk
Our bodies attached like Siamese twins.
The stench of tulips, weather a monochrome.

Who could endure paradise a week?

You refuse a last strawberry, and I say,
I say, "Please God invent something new."
You say, "No, not God. *You* invent a new paradise."

I roll my mind out to a runway,
Adjust our seatbelts, the engines shriek.
You say, "I'm afraid," We lift, up, up.
You say, "All I can see is clouds."

Our paradise is clouds. "Clouds?" Yes, clouds.

◆

Distance

In this country everything is so far apart:
Parents in Utah, children in Florida.
It's so vast it takes days by car to cross
Or bushels of money for a jet; and Alaska
Way up there and Hawaii way, way out there.
Take us at breakfast: You seem to be in L.A.,
I in New York, my coffee cup in Kansas.
My hand disappears from view. I can't see it
Any more than I can see you. Where are you
Across the table? Where are you?

✦

Lost

It's hard for me to get lost in this town
But I try. I seem to know all the streets
And paths. Yes, even where no streetlights are:
At night I can find my way, can name the lanes
Without signs, name the sleepers in their houses,
The dead who built them. How can I get lost?

I try to get lost, to take a wrong turn
That leads to a strange street, an unknown house
Where I ring a bell. The door creaks open
An inch. I say, "I'm lost, very lost."
A voice answers in a tongue I do not know.
I rejoice. At last I am on the threshold
Of the unknown, unexplored. I am lost.

But then a car pulls up to the curbstone
And familiar voices call. "Hey there.
There he is. We found him." They found me.

◆

Please Write: Don't Phone

While there is mail there is hope.
After we have hung up I can't recall
Your words, and your voice sounds strange
Whether from distance, a bad cold, deceit
I don't know. When you call I'm asleep
Or bathing or my mouth is full of toast.

I can't think of what to say.
"We have rain"? "We have snow"?

Let us write instead: surely our fingers spread out
With pen on paper touch more of the mind's flesh
Than the sound waves moving from throat to lips
To phone, through wire, to one ear.
I can touch the paper you touch.
I can see you undressed in your calligraphy.
I can read you over and over.
I can read you day after day.
I can wait at the mailbox with my hair combed,
In my best suit.
I hang up. What did you say?
What did you say? Your phone call is gone.
I hold the envelope you addressed in my hand.
I hold the skin that covers you.

✦

Panthers at the Sherry Netherland Hotel

They leap from the ledge thirty floors up.
Panthers on all sides so high above

The street you don't see them. Or if you do,
If you by chance look up, you are not sure

What you see: greyhounds? panthers? stone or bronze?
Ah, they are panthers, green bronze panthers.

Why are they placed almost out of sight?
Why forever jumping toward the sky?

And why after years of passing have I
Never seen them, never looked up that high?

Then I looked still higher, above the ledge,
Where I saw a tower. See! See! from the top

Of the tower are more panthers that leap,
Nine more panthers radiate like spokes.

I don't understand why they are there.
Most of what is seems outside my vision

Or if I at last see what has been hidden
I seldom know what it is that I see.

I had a vision of bronze panthers;
All night they leap at the roof of my mind.

✦

God as Magician

He yanks a whole Spring out of his top hat
Of night: warm air, leaves, violets, daffodils.
Or maybe wraps up the town in ice.

His wand moves and children tumble from wombs.
Or he makes things disappear, say grandfathers
And snow, entire cities under volcanoes . . .

He palmed the universe out of his sleeve
Like a grenade, exploding it "bang,"
A giant Fourth of July rocket. Behold,

Our earth, the heavens, the beautiful debris
Still soaring beyond telescopes, beyond. . . .
It beats me. You flew, a bouquet from his wand

To me as I flew. I love you, I say
Before he tucks us with his wand away.

✦

Henry Flagler's Song

I invented Florida when I was old.
We lived in New York City in the cold.

I was retired from oil, I had some wealth;
Mary, my first wife, was in poor health.

We rode in my private railroad car.
Ah, the warm south surely would be her cure.

That winter we steamed into Jacksonville
Where I drew up Florida like my will:

I said I would bequeath to future men
Of wealth and station a temperate garden

By the sea which they could reach by yacht or rail
Where they could toast the sun with ginger ale.

Now in my holy city of St. Augustine,
My hotel Ponce de Leon can be seen:

Its many courts and cool retreats with fountains,
Water spraying from the mouths of dolphins.

That my civilization would prevail,
That all Florida could be coasted by rail

I built my roadbeds, bridges down the entire state.
Now its length my hotels punctuate.

My conquest is a land of orange trees,
Palms, bougainvillaea, and warm salt seas.

After God, as artist, I have created most and best:
St. Augustine, Palm Beach, Miami, Key West.

It did not matter much that Mary died;
In Florida I found a younger bride.

◆

Among Churches

Surely if at any spot in the city
A spirit in seriousness should descend,
It would be here on the corner of Greene
And Fisher, and should hover over my bed.

My neighbors are three churches, a synagogue,
A funeral home. Processions of dead
Flow past my window daily to our
Cemetery out of view four blocks west.

Serious possessors of expensive cars
Curb them under the Sunday morning bells.
While I feed on the seven course Sunday
Daily News, I know that prayers must rise:

Yes, thousands and thousands on all four sides.
Surely a diagram of intersecting
Holy forces from church to church would pin
The Holy Ghost above my uncombed head.

Yet wings swirling like a helicopter's,
A figure lowered, swaying on a rope,
These do not occur. And I never venture
Outdoors to look roofward. I know I'll see . . .

Nothing, squirrels or a real helicopter
Stuttering between steeples. The Spirit
Here is hidden as in shopping malls
Or golf links, or bars that open at one.

But the dailiness of dead hauled off
Regally in Cadillac hearses, and then
The thousands of cars parked on Sunday,
These make me think. Of what I am not sure.

What might quadrangulate on the corner
Of Greene and Fisher over my Sunday news,
Skydive down on the roof over my head
Has not. Next week, who knows? I like it here:

A glint of rose glass, puffs of organ music.
I'd be more serious about all this
If I could. Anyway I like the neighborhood.
It's safe, quiet, and nothing happens here.

✦

A Good Life

Memories of a good life are not enough;
The fade out begins. I run to beat the dark,
I swim to light my eyes. I give up drink,
I diet on yogurt, squash seeds, herbal tea.

I take the lotus position, meditate.
Arising I fly straight at the new day
(What's done, was done); make the new day
Fresh as home baked bread, blueberries bog ripe,
Clams dug, steamed the same hour. My mind receptive
As a child's. Yes, I could wish for hail storms,
A city in flames, a hovering harem,
A visit from an angel. No, I train
For a different kind of tomorrow today.
I run to beat the dark, I swim to light my eyes,
To see the usual I have passed by.

I need a vision: Let me see an apple
That is tart, firm from a tree, an orchard
In Vermont, an orchard in winter snowfall,
The orchard blank as a white sheet of paper.
I walk in this snow. It squeaks in sub-zero.

I will not look over my shoulder, behind
At my footsteps, at the disrupted snow.
I am not ready yet to be the past in the past.

✦

Island of Bones

On this island
The island of bones
Dogs bark, fighting cocks crow
Cats cry and the winds blow
In from the sea

I awake on my patio
Under the palm trees and mango
Odor of aloe on the wind
Iced lime water by my side
In the warm south Keats yearned for.
It is always summer in the Keys
I sleep much and float in the warm
Buoyant waters of my dream.

See come, come sea, she waver, buoy banger
Tart water, fish full, piss warm:
Yellow tail, snapper, angels, eel, squid.
Voices blow from the pier, twist in salt air
Out to sea, he come, she come, air in sail,
Sun shimmer, surf silver, bodies roast
In oil. The pelicans dive for fish
"Gua gua, gua gua," the little boys yell. "Hey puta."
The hulls of shrimpers glide toward
The Marquesas, the Dry Tortugas to Cozumel.

She lies on her back in a pink bikini
She removes the top
He kneels rubbing Copper Tone
Into her thighs.
"What's your name?" she asks him.

Down, down, down into the neverwhere
Shed of all the above
Through coral canyons, pink sea fans
I dive to a new world, swim for my cure
With barracuda, tarpon, shrimp, sea horses, rays . . .

In 1622 the *Atocha* sank
A hurricane cracked it on a coral reef
Its 20 bronze cannon were no defense
Against the pirates of air and sea.
In the Archivo de las Indias
Documents say the *Atocha,*
A sailing bank vault, held
903 silver ingots
255,000 silver coins
161 pieces of gold bullion
47 troy tons of treasure
50 feet below the sea
30 miles from the Island of Bones.

Finders keepers, losers weepers.
The fire chief's red car
Runs cocaine from bar to bar.

"I take my enemies' names, write them down
On paper, put it in freezing compartment.
One enemy threw guinea peppers on
My porch. All are powerless, all frozen now.
My husband was seeing another woman.
I take one of his crotch hairs and make knots
In it, then drop it in that vase up there.
He's impotent now, can't do it to her
Or me. Go. I can't tell you more."

Down, down, down,
I've fallen down the coast
From Maine to the very end
From ice-floes and snow drifts,
I've reached the southern end of land.
America's end, my own end.
In northern winters, the ground frozen
The blood frozen month after month,
I dreamt of warm water and palms.

"Hiss, spaugh, squeak.
Honey an effen tire's flat.
Now the fish is in the fat.
Jeez I've got to take a leak.
Splat, hiss, splat, dribble.
Watch out for coconuts.
Where's all the other people?
O.K, O.K, let's jack it up.
Clump up, clump up, clump up
Clump up, clump up, clump up.
Hey come back! After all I paid
For her drinks and never got . . .
Sssssssssssssssssssss wump.
Blue light, blue light, blue light!
Snap, crackle, pop.
Club, cuffs, squat, search.
Hi ya cop."

A tour train circles the island town
The tourists buy straw hats and shells.

"Getting it up is no sweat
It's finding the right piece
To get it up for into down, right?"

Down, down, down.

"Well ya see it was this way
Bill and I was in Howie's bar flat broke
And Bill says, 'See the nigger in the booth
He's a pusher like he's got dough
So turn him on.' Like I'm to ball him
While Bill grabs all his bread
But soon's he gets it in me
Bill gives him the old boom boom
I don't know why in the head.
One dead nigger.
Cops got us on the seven miles bridge.
Yeh twenty bucks but I won't swallow it."

Down, down, down, in that swinging old town.

"For four years chicken farming was my life
Until I learned to dive. I don't know
Why a man with a wife, four children would
Decide to dive for treasure. You say money.
Yes, of course, but I'd say the adventure
Like climbing unclimbed mountain peaks. My name
Is Fisher. I live out my name. I live
Like an inverted astronaut. Down, down, down
To the bottom of the sea among wrecks.
I am an archaeologist of sorts.
If I believed in Atlantis I would
Find Atlantis. I knew the *Atocha*
Sank 350 years ago.
For 12 years I've swept the ocean floor,
My boats logged 120,000 miles,
I've spent 2,500,000 bucks.
When at night my boat the Northwind last year
Sank Dirk, my son, Angela, his wife, drowned …
It was Dirk who found the nine bronze cannon
Raised two and died. Some gold we've found, the bulk
Still lies nearby under sand I'll blast away.
By October I'll be rich. Here is a gold chalice.
"This is a boatswain's whistle."

My Night Blooming Cactus
Is twenty feet tall.
Its buds, fist big, appear in June.
The flowers open only at night
When the moon is full.
My pale yellow flowers shine
For one night, for only one night
Then close at dawn and die.

Down, down, down.
It's rapture time
Under the frangipani tree.
Whee. Whee. We.
I'll go down on you
You go down on me.
Mangoes, fresh mangoes
Get your mangoes here.

In the deep of my mind all things swim
Can I in my own deep find a rapture
And return to the surface, to the rim
Of the world where you await my capture
With coffee and the daily newspaper?

Down, down, down.
It's rapture time on the Keys.
Now for the weather:
The temperature is eighty-five degrees,
Out of the south a ten mile wind,
Waves are two feet inside the reef,
Three beyond the reef.
Today will be clear and sunny,
Now it's rapture time at the Pro Dive Shop,
Best deal on diving lessons in the Keys.
So pop right out for this week's sale on wet suits.
Remember: Key West divers do it deeper.

I bicycle from one ocean to another,
From the Atlantic to the Gulf, ten minutes
Coast to Coast. At El Casique
I eat arroz con pollo with black beans
And bread. Spanish crackles in the air.
I don't understand one word.
I didn't want to get up today:
I lay in bed counting the girls I've made,
On one hand.
The sea of my mind is cloudy, its bottom
Stirred up. Weeds float on the top.
To live on memory is to live on tea and Jell-o,
Yet blind with hope and cups of coffee
I cycle from sea to sea.

KEY LIME PIE
Combine 4 egg yolks
⅓ cup lime juice
One can condensed milk
Pour into graham-cracker crust
Add whipped cream
Serve chilled.

"It's a matter of energy and space.
Today I've had an energy loss.
I live in such a little space
I have no money, no job, all day
In welfare offices, the county shrink,
Enrolling my son in day camp . . . he steals.
It's space, the narrowing of space we live in, love on.

My Baptist mother ran away to Oregon
To cure drunks at missions. She died
Of cancer at forty-two, but I'd say
She died from lack of space. She was a prude.
I paid my way through college with my body.
It's hard for me to get through to men;
Even the nicest want me in their beds.
I don't mind dying. I'm suicidal.
It's only the body, body space when
Mind space is where God can come through.
I know I look twenty-five, but I'm thirty-two."

I sit here wishing for wishes
In the Pier House bar
Where I can see the shrimp boats
At the cocktail hour
And where movie stars play in the pool.

"Get your mangoes here
Fresh watermelon, bananas,
Roasted peanuts, conch salad,
Conch salad makes you horny
And when you're hot you're hot."

Everyone clapped when the sun went down
And the clouds went up in flame.

✦

The Great Wall

Whether it was to keep them out or us inside
  We don't know.
Whether they built it or we built it
  No one recalls.
But here it lies mile after mile of grey stone.

The wall is twenty feet high and six feet thick
  With no gates.
Behind both sides are towers where armed guards watch
  Day and night.
We have savage dogs and spotlights for darkness.
  No one can cross.

We are told that behind the wall plagues spread like fire.
We are told that the people there are ignorant and cruel.
We are told that they are filthy and poor,
  that they would kill our men
  that they would rape our women
  that they would devour our children.
We are told that they are unbelievers,
  that they speak in a strange and guttural tongue,
  that they are infested with lice.

I live in a hut on a small square of soil.
I have built a fence around my plot.
I keep the gates locked day and night.
My dog is hungry and savage.

When I raise my voice my wife stands still.
She never speaks: I don't know what she thinks
  nor have I ever.
When we go to bed at night she sleeps on her side,
  her back toward me rigid as stone.

◆

Dogs

I hear them bark outside my window, dogs
The country is going to, packs of them,
Rabid dogs, plunging through forest and field,
Our city streets at night, leaping at doors,
At each others' throats, at our throats. I've heard
About them all my years. Daytimes they are
Behind fences, chained in yards, locked in barns.
And in daylight they wag tails, lick our hands.
Nights on the loose, howling they race in packs.

Midnight this tumult calls me to the window
Where outside in moonlight I see my neighbor
Unlock his gate. He looks long-eared and furry.
I hear him growl, snap his jaws. I bark back.

✦

Second-Hand Mattress

This yard sale mattress, clean
  And smelling fresh,
Is king-sized, smooth and deep
  And taut. I feel
Just looking at it sleep
  Drift in my eyes
On this warm June afternoon.

No one is looking. I take
  A plunge and drop
Down on its springy top,
  Stretch out my legs.
A languor settles over
  My clouding eyes,
An amorous fog rolls in.

Think, all the lovers who
  Have dallied here,
All the bodies refreshed
  By sleep and love,
By dreams of fame and wealth:
  Cars, horses, yachts.
What is better than this,

This mattress in a yard?
  I open my
Eyes, look around at objects
  On display: plates,
A toaster, picture frames,
  Three wooden chairs,
A box of books, a rug.

Why all this stuff for sale?
  Are they parting
With odds and ends they have
  Replaced with finer
Goods? Are they moving to
  A smaller house
Because they've overspent?

Divorce? That could be it:
    Sell all they've bought
Together and shared,
    The mattress least
Wanted of all they've owned
    Where in the dark
They've touched with shame or hate.

Perhaps the owner lay
    For months in pain
And died where now I sprawl.
    My head spins: love,
Birth, deceit and death—
    Murder, suicide—
All possible on this soft

Surface where I stretch out,
    and see above
The yard the vacant puzzle
    Of sky.
There nothing is bought or sold.
    I sneeze, stand up.
There's nothing here I want to buy.

✦

Judgment Day at the Library

A tremor of earth at midnight wakes
The books, another blasts them from their shelves
Until they lie scattered in the stacks.

"It's Judgment Day," the Bibles joyfully shout.
A sprawling geological treatise
Replies, "You black backed fools, it's an earthquake."

"No! War," says General Pershing. "That's a bomb.
Everyone that's up lie flat on the floor.
Be calm. In moments our fighter squads will come."

Whatever caused the books to fall as thick
As Milton's disobedient Angels fell
To Hell's floor from Heaven was not yet known.

Upturned, dishevelled on spines, jackets open,
More dazed than hurt, after the first moment
Unshelved they mutter in their anarchic state.

"It's been years since I've moved from my shelf space.
No one's checked me out, clutched me, heard my words.
I'm happy now under Caesar on the floor."

"Poor you. I'm seldom here. I'm out with men,"
A coquette says. "They like to hold me tight.
How I'll be missed. I have a waiting list."

"I have been out and alas was overdue.
Those strange hands at my frontispiece I hate.
I'd rather lie here in dust than circulate."

"All wisdom of mankind was sewn within
My leaves," a supine philosopher complains.
"Call me a binder, I'm split to the brains."

"Your mind was always addled with ideas.
No cure," a boldfaced historian says.
"Those who live by the sword have the last word."

Lucifer rejoices in this disordered state.
"The past is all mistakes, so blast again,
Explode the library, make a clean slate."

At last their Supreme Being speaks, "O books,
Who by unhappy chance fell from your fixed
Numerical places to messy heaps,

It is your Judgment Day. Too many books
Now crowd the stacks, too many seldom read
Or never, too many old beyond repair,

Or lewd, or holding unsound views.
My censors will decide which of you we
Will restore and which to burn in furnace flame."

✦

The Melodeon

At the melodeon her mother sang
While outside on the tennis court the ball
Her brothers struck, plock plock, across the net . . .
Applause by father from astride his horse,
    Clap, clap.

At the melodeon an aunt pumped out
Her wedding march while outside her brothers
Tied streamers to the hired marriage car.
The silver presents from their boxes gleamed,
    Hurray, hurray.

At the melodeon my mother sang
Next to the coffin where her father lay.
Outside the tennis court was cracked with weeds.
Her brothers bowed their white haired heads and coughed
    Good-bye, good-bye.

At the melodeon with bellows that leak
The auctioneer entreats the crowd for bids
Upon the tennis court that is no more
Behind the shabby house the wreckers bought.
    Tick tock, tick, tock.

✦

Nomads

There are people who live nowhere
Long enough to be from anyplace
Nameable, to whom moving is always
Improvement. Good-bye, good-bye, they say.
They're off to Vancouver or Maine,
Or wherever they've never seen.
On arrival they study maps:
How to go from Bangor to Butte.
Ah Butte, Butte! In Bangor they tune
The engine, work odd jobs for gas.

There are people who live on highways
Looking for whatever is next.
In Canaveral rockets are fueling,
A map of the planets at hand.
Good-bye Bangor. Good-bye Butte.
They are off. The earth is the size
Of a tennis ball, then a marble,
A period. Good-bye, good-bye.

✦

A Balloon Rises

God thinks in numbers,
not words.

The higher we go the less we see
Below. So it is with thought:

When my mind moves up from one brown cow,
With a tail flicking flies from
His twitching flank, to a herd of twenty
In a fenced green field, I no
Longer see the flies that bite.

Now higher and higher I float until
I see four hundred specks
In one sea of green: the one brown cow
Is gone. Below clouds drift
Between my eyes and the fields of green.

My mind divides four hundred by a score:
That is what I think, twenty, pure 20.
The balloon sinks to the field below where
Tess dreaming milks a cow—all that sensual
Delight, ensuing pain. She swats a fly.

✦

The Cure

When I have told all to my analyst
And lie empty, my life hissed out . . .
The luminous dial on my bedside clock
Ticks out its sentence: empty hours, empty years.
I shrink. The hands of the clock grow
Arms of a blacksmith. Striking, striking.
One. One. One. Two. Two. Two.
I am nothing but a collapsed balloon.
My bladder empty, not a drop.
My doctor has cured me of everything.
Three. It's three. It's four. It's five.
I arise at seven, bathe, shave.
Today I wear my glen plaid suit.
Everyone at the office will note how fit
I look, a fit cover for a book
Of blank pages. A thief, my analyst,
Has robbed me of my past. Come pain.
I breathe deeply, inhale the rich
Polluted air. Misery is everywhere.

✦

Two Models in a Studio

We are nude and pose as divers.
The artist must invent the sea,
The fish, a noontime sky above.

Our breaths held, heads down we stare
At fish, yellow, purple, red, blue.
Above us sailboats skim the waves.

Airplanes float through clouds while
We swim down, deeper, deeper down.
What is our goal? We don't know.

Do we dive for shells, treasure ships,
Or only the feel of salt water
On skin and hair? We don't know.

I push through the sea without thought,
Without mask, tank or fins or spear
Past fire coral, down dark fathoms

Where unseen the mind's monsters swim
With monsters of the sea. Air gone,
We surface, she and I, and dress.

Here is the painting of divers
The artist made: A man, woman
And bright tropical fish, a canvas

Of blue water, blue sky above,
No sting rays, no sharks, no moral
Of good or evil, no menace here

Only a naked man and woman
Diving into a foreign element,
A perfect ephemeral blue.

✦

The Uncertainty Principle

From my captain's chair in the yard
I steer the earth among the stars.

Inside the house my wife's asleep.
Our hall clock ticks out minutes, hours.

A cloudless autumn night outdoors
For sailing through the universe.

All thoughts of civic duty gone
Or right or wrong I travel on.

I am not Noah riding a flood
With all the birds and beasts aboard,

Nor am I Ulysses awash
In interstellar seas.

I do not search for gold or for
The waters of eternal youth.

Unmindful of my past I sail
Through chandeliers of planets

In search of what I do not know.
The universe swells like a balloon

After the big bang that began
It all. Before the crunch that marks

The end, I'd like to be certain
Of where I am and what is where.

✦

My Father Breaks His Hip at Eighty-One

You are right not to like the nurse
Who calls you "sweetie"
And right to hate the food and curse
The bad men who
Tied you up for no good reason.

Where are you? In the hospital.
They've strapped you down
Because you try to run away.
I'm not your father.
What next? Why home, where you belong.

Your mind is numb from drugs you're fed
To blot the pain,
The surgeons have installed a new
Right hip socket.
The wound will close and heal: you'll walk.

"Not my hip, it's my mind that's broken."
"Sweetie, sweetie."
The nurse removes your dinner tray,
Clamps your restraints.
You disappear under the sheets.

All six feet four of you wrestles
    In the bedclothes.
You move, tied up and drugged, nowhere . . .
    "Sweetie, sweetie."
You will walk soon the doctors say.

The hospital rests on a plateau
    Under green hills.
Above them are pillows of clouds.
    I leave your room.
In the parking lot I name my children's names.

Father who in black judge's robes
    Judged us all
With fairness and swift certitude
    You have in mind
And body failed. Lord raise you up.

✦

Teresa and the Spear of Time

I

Though unmoving they seem to rise as clouds
Under the piercing bars of light that fall
Upon their forms and they seem oblivious
To their place upon a stage raised above
The diners at their meal, oblivious to
Occupants of boxes right and left who
Whisper and ignore these two as if they
Were invisible in their ascent
Into the dome and who ignore all pain
And passion flashing in the shafts of light.

II

The boy who holds the spear in his right hand,
His arm cocked back, stands at her side while he
Touches her right shoulder with his left hand,
Smiles at her, a sweet smile. His wings are still.
Has he already thrust the spear and then
Withdrawn it? Or has he yet to thrust it
Into her chest? We do not know. His hair
Flames in curls. His wings are light as fire.

The woman, half-reclining, floats in waves
Of the robe that covers her form, a robe
That ripples and swirls in liquid tumult.
Only her face, her hands and feet are bare.
The fingers of her left hand dangle at
Her side. Do her curled right hand fingers beckon
To the smiting, bare-chested boy with wings?

Her eyes are closed or half-closed, her mouth open
In a gasp, sigh or cry. Her nostrils flare.
She seems neither awake nor asleep, does
Not move or speak, hears, if at all, whispers
Outside her body's wall. Her pain is beyond
Endurance and yet is delectable, bearable
And unbearable under the gold shafts of light.

The spear still rests in the boy's right hand.
His left still lifts her robe at her shoulder.
The boy, girlish in curls, still smiles down
A conquering smile at the helpless woman.

III

All lines of perception meet in her form
Where her moment of glorious pain—
Inflicted by the boy who is no boy,
Who holds the spear of time in suspense,
Time suspended in white marble for all
These centuries since Bernini remade the saint
In marble flowing like a frozen stream
Under the metal bars of yellow light—
Where her moment of pain is without time
And without end. Above a skyscape
Of clouds and angels whirl in paint
Toward the dove at the top, and below
The diners at their supper turn to bronze,
The men in boxes to stone, and beneath
Two skeletons on marble pavement dance.

✦

Watson on the Beach

Some custom stronger than church-going wheels us each summer
From city to shore where we strip habits of the year,
Declare bodies for sun, tides to wash.
We arrive not knowing why we came, except for change;
As last year, years before, an uncle less, a child more—the same.

I
I squat on skeletons spat from the sea;
Stare at water, water's dead.
Near mounds of jellyfish, my flesh
Bears all the puffy age I dread,
Yet an asteroid in my hand retains its points
And clams can stuff their flesh inside their bones,
Then lock their joints.
Tough luck I am a man
So gone to flesh. I do what I can:
Provide my young shovels and a kite;
Let them dig to China, that old world,
Or string a new one in the sky. My son
Wades in to engineer the next world in sand,
Then buries me up to my chin
And rides, a conqueror, on my head.
All life squats on powdery skulls of the dead.

II
My body underground, I search for the horizon,
And see only a blur of fog that screens the edge;
Yet who can mark where beach or sea begins?
Death and life meet in this gray smear,
Shift, cross, for a moment, as lovers, are the same.

My eyes close: a wrong turn
Off the highway, a dark dead end.
My motor fails, mind goes flat.
I wait for the giant wrecker to come,
Find and tow me home.

I wait listening: a shell,
I hold myself to my ear,
Yet I hear nothing
But motors of the sea,
Wheels quarreling
Before wheels of man.

At last my ears attune,
All quarrels turn to song,
And string sounds rise, pour in waves:
Sounds fill me until only sound exists—
Sound sun and stars once made,
And light recorded on our sea
Is now replayed from water's memory,
Record of our seed in sound,
Around, around,
World lost, world found.

Do dead stars fallen from their tracks,
Extinguished notes, heaped shells
On dead ends of the universe
Fill with water's sound, the past, their past within,
Fill until they are nothing yet everything,
Audible motion that will never still?

God grows in my ear's shell;
His toenail pokes my skull.

But Watson,
Holding a starfish in your hand,
You are no star and never were.
You are no one in particular.
What son, indeed? What seed?
Your name will never tell.
You are everything and an empty shell.
What son begat Watson begat Watson?
A seed, a pod, a sound,
And one by one they drowned.
Dogs and sonar towers on the beach
Hear sounds your ears will never reach.

O Watson is dead, but he will rise
Wearing starfish instead of eyes.

III

A detonation in the world above, a flame.
Has the last excavation begun?
Does the wrecker finally come
With chain and hoist?
Gentle music, water in my ear,
The universe leaks out.

It is the young, lolling on treacherous sand
With portable radios to moor them to land.
From their center a girl springs elastic flesh
Between me and the Atlantic
Which she smothers.
She watches shore to see who watches her.
This girl's flesh resurrects me from my grave.
I overthrow my son; he tumbles from my head.
Shall I cartwheel across the sand and dive?

Stop! Back to your grave old man
So run to flesh.
You held the universe like change
In pockets of your ears.
Spend all that for her? Too late. Too late.
In male form, young and beautiful as she,
A lifeguard come to rescue
Jumps between her and me.

In looking from their flesh to ours,
I see we have a kind of beauty too:
Ignore a line off plumb, a blur,
My wife and I are beautiful as they.
The swimming mackerel cannot tell,
I'm sure, one human swimmer from another.

A camera clicks; my body is immortal;
My jellied flesh flies to the lens.
Flattened and dried, transformed to celluloid,
It will project over screens in future years
The same: Between children and wife
Back to land, squinting out to sea,
A man stands stripped to his loins.

IV
The sea rolls in white-sheeted sleep;
Motions my flesh to its cold bed
In which I sink, shivering,
Open-eyed, a figure in a dream,
The sea's dream of itself.
Deep in its mind
I swim toward darkness,

A sunken island
That at night when I swim in sleep
Seems at bottom of sleep,
Yet awake I cannot recall
Ever docking at that island
We think submerged,
That island which may, as memory,
Be a mirror on the floor
Where waver from above the sea
What grains of light
Wheel spinning through topless space
And wheeling each grain is
A broiling contention that is a star,
Wild in self war as war on space.

Projected on a screen
I saw once what was no dream:
Wind rip water,
Water a burning ship
Shelled by a submarine;
A sailor wheel, stab his mate,
And jump to the one last lifeboat seat.

Wind, water, fire accelerate
What gas of space began,
And man must imitate
A glass that lightning makes of sand.

Fish swoop
At hull,
At porthole glass,
At eyes behind a beating fist now still,

At burning eyes,
Green mirrors of stars,
Sodden flames that hum
What we know at heart, the heart.
Black Angels unseen in night now pass
His bubbles of eyes burnt down to gas.

Bless eyes of Robert Wright,
Fog on some ocean island's floor.
Bless Charles Stretch, bless Hartmut Arntz,
Who died from war.
Bless my parents, grandparents
Watson, Trimble, Swett, Berdan,
Back to where we all began;
And back again:
My wife, my son, my daughter,
Their progeny and me.
Bless solids, liquids, gas,
Whatever comes, to pass.

My thoughts plunge below,
Swarm in rows around the sunken hull
Swept under the sea's rug, under its bed.
Ears popping, all air consumed I waken,
Rise awkward as a submarine,
Above my own the ocean's dream.
Too deep for me this foreign element.

V
I ride breakers,
Wade out again,
Swing through creation,

All past, the sun
Wheel back and out
And back again
Until all motion,
Time,
I am its pendulum.

The sea coughs,
Spits in space;
I splatter beachward
On my face.

Rest, rider, rest.
Bring fried clams and beer,
Ointments, tape, towels.
Bring sleep, bring girls.
And under an umbrella a woman
Changes; from her bodice drops
A fallen heaven of pearls,
Pearls of my catechism: sleep.
Immortal flesh picked clean,
Immortal mind drained,
Awash I sleep in sun.

VI
The bladder of fog over our horizon
Inflates as a dirigible, swells
Over beach, over us.
Sun, water, sand, lifeguard, girl
Of elastic flesh—all flesh,
Drawn as dust in a vacuum cleaner,
Become grey gas within its sides,

Ghosts in dust of vacant house,
Shuttered, chairs in shrouds.
All voices, voices on a telephone,
Unanswered, a buzzing sound and gone.
Our family, hand in hand, drifts
Over invisible earth toward light,
Where we specters turn to flesh
In our bath house on the parking lot.

Air that pumped the fog so huge
Between the sun and sand,
Now sucks all fog away.

VII
Under blankets on dunes we watch the townsmen
Wheel new worlds of fire against the night's,
Pump rockets in its side, explode all dark.
They light a bonfire with ten tons of sticks,
A thousand rubber tires, on top a boat.
Tonight they scorch the sky that scorches us.
A marching band with drum sticks flays in time
The ashen skin of air.
While children dance in orbits on the sand,
Above the wind that blew the fog away
Blows out our stars: A puff, a hiss, they drown.
Our flag of liquid fire drops, self-devoured, down.

The boat sinks to its crematorium;
Cars with sleeping children wheel toward home
Where we shall bed, boarded and bricked
From all elements but one,
That all I father, O father, and the sea fathers
Are: Fog flows past our screens, the glass,
Brings, through our window frame, a burning boat.

Independence Day, Nauset Beach

Index of First Lines and Titles